DISCOVER DOGS WITH THE AMERICAN CANINE ASSOCIATION

I LIKE BERNESE MOUNTAIN DOGS!

Linda Bozzo

It is the mission of the American Canine Association (ACA) to provide registered dog owners with the educational support needed for raising, training, showing, and breeding the healthiest pets expected by responsible pet owners throughout the world. Through our activities and services, we encourage and support the dog world in order to promote best-known husbandry standards as well as to ensure that the voice and needs of our customers are quickly and properly addressed.

Our continued support, commitment, and direction are guided by our customers, including veterinary, legal, and legislative advisors. ACA aims to provide the most efficient, cooperative, and courteous service to our customers and strives to set the standard for education and problem solving for all who depend on our services.

For more information, please visit www.acacanines.com, e-mail customerservice@acadogs.com, phone 1-800-651-8332, or write to the American Canine Association at PO Box 121107, Clermont, FL 34712.

Published in 2018 by Enslow Publishing, LLC.
101 W. 23rd Street, Suite 240, New York, NY 10011

Library of Congress Cataloging-in-Publication Data

Names: Bozzo, Linda, author.
Title: I like Bernese mountain dogs!/Linda Bozzo.
Description: New York : Enslow Publishing, 2018. | Series: Discover dogs with the American Canine Association | Includes bibliographical references and index. | Audience: Grades K to 3.
Identifiers: LCCN 2017001303| ISBN 9780766086364 (library-bound) | ISBN 9780766088740 (pbk.) | ISBN 9780766088689 (6-pack)
Subjects: LCSH: Bernese mountain dog—Juvenile literature.
Classification: LCC SF429.B47 B69 2017 | DDC 636.73—dc23
LC record available at https://lccn.loc.gov/2017001303

Printed in the United States of America

To Our Readers: We have done our best to make sure all websites in this book were active and appropriate when we went to press. However, the author and the publisher have no control over and assume no liability for the material available on those websites or on any websites they may link to. Any comments or suggestions can be sent by e-mail to customerservice@enslow.com.

Photo Credits: Cover, p. 1 Erik Lam/Shutterstock.com; p. 3 (left) Grigorita Ko/Shutterstock.com; p. 3 (right) DragoNika/Shutterstock.com; p. 5 Juniors Bildarchiv GmbH/Alamy Stock Photo; p. 6 Kzenon/Shutterstock.com; p. 9 Tatiana Murr/Shutterstock.com; p. 10 Jill Lehmann Photography/Moment Open/Getty Images; p. 13 (left) Zuzule/Shutterstock.com; p. 13 (collar) graphicphoto/iStock/Thinkstock, (bed) Luisa Leal Photography/Shutterstock.com, (brush) gvictoria/Shutterstock.com, (food and water bowls) exopixel/Shutterstock.com, (leash, toys) © iStockphoto.com/Liliboas; p. 14 Portland Press Herald/Getty Images; p. 17 H. Mark Weidman Photography/Alamy Stock Photo; p. 18 Dima Sidelnikov/Shutterstock.com; p. 19 Vanessa van Rensburg/Shutterstock.com; p. 21 mgs/Moment Open/Getty Images.

Enslow Publishing
101 W. 23rd Street
Suite 240
New York, NY 10011
USA
enslow.com

CONTENTS

IS A BERNESE MOUNTAIN DOG RIGHT FOR YOU?

Bernese mountain dogs, also known as **Berners**, make great family pets. Though large in size, they are gentle dogs. If you live on a large piece of land, the Berner may be right for you.

In the early 1900s, Bernese mountain dogs were often used for pulling carts to the local markets.

A DOG OR A PUPPY?

Berner puppies like to learn. But training any puppy takes time. If you do not have time to train a puppy, an older Berner may be better for your family.

Bernese puppies grow into powerful dogs.

LOVING YOUR BERNESE MOUNTAIN DOG

Love your Bernese mountain dog by keeping him busy. Play with him. Teach him tricks. He will like being by your side.

EXERCISE

Berners enjoy long walks or hikes on a **leash**.

Berners like to play games, like **fetch**.

Bernese mountain dogs are cold-weather dogs. They enjoy playing in the snow.

FEEDING YOUR BERNESE MOUNTAIN DOG

Bernese mountain dogs can be fed wet or dry dog food. Ask a **veterinarian (vet)**, a doctor for animals, which food is best for your dog and how much to feed her. Give your Berner fresh, clean water every day.

Remember to keep your dog's food and water dishes clean. Dirty dishes can make a dog sick.

Do not feed your dog people food. It can make her sick.

Your new dog will need:

a collar with a tag

a bed

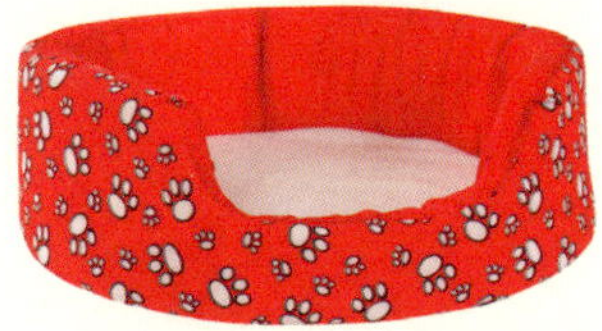

a brush

food and water dishes

a leash

toys

Berners have coats with three colors: black, white, and tan.

GROOMING

Bernese mountain dogs **shed** all year long. This means their hair falls out all the time. They should be brushed often to keep them clean and looking their best.

Your dog will need a bath every so often. Use a gentle soap made just for dogs.

A Berner's nails need to be clipped. A vet or **groomer** can show you how. Your dog's ears should be cleaned, and her teeth should be brushed by an adult.

WHAT YOU SHOULD KNOW

Bernese mountain dogs get along with most other pets. But if bored, Berners can get into trouble. Berners are not best for first-time dog owners.

Because of health problems, Berners don't live as long as some other breeds. They usually only live six to eight years.

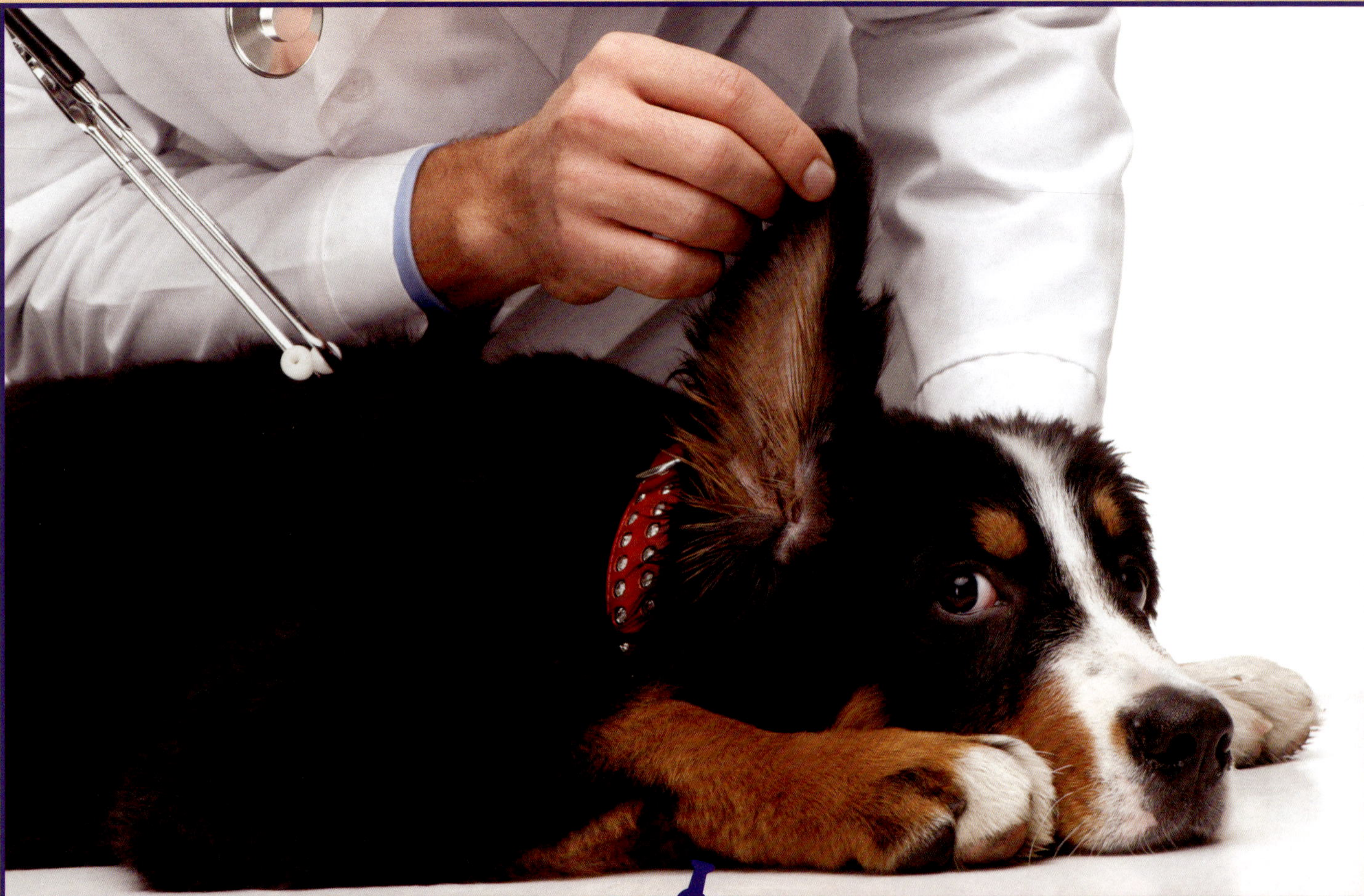

You will need to take your new dog to the vet for a checkup. He will need shots, called **vaccinations**, and yearly checkups to keep him healthy. If you think your dog may be sick or hurt, call your vet.

A GOOD FRIEND

Your Bernese mountain dog will be a good friend to everyone he meets.

Most Berners don't mind strangers.

NOTE TO PARENTS

It is important to consider having your dog spayed or neutered when the dog is young. Spaying and neutering are operations that prevent unwanted puppies and can help improve the overall health of your dog.

It is also a good idea to microchip your dog, in case he or she gets lost. A vet will implant a microchip under the skin containing an identification number that can be scanned at a vet's office or animal shelter. The microchip registry is contacted, and the company uses the ID number to look up your information from a database.

Some towns require licenses for dogs, so be sure to check with your town clerk.

For more information, speak with a vet.

There are many dogs, young and old, waiting to be adopted from animal shelters and rescue groups.

Words to Know

Berner Another name for a Bernese mountain dog.

fetch To go after a toy and bring it back.

groomer A person who bathes and brushes dogs.

leash A chain or strap that attaches to a dog's collar.

shed When dog hair falls out so new hair can grow.

vaccinations Shots that dogs need to stay healthy.

veterinarian (vet) A doctor for animals.

Read About Dogs

Books

Morey, Allan. *Bernese Mountain Dogs* (Big Dogs). North Mankato, MN: Capstone Press, 2016.

Wheeler, Jill C. *Bernese Mountain Dogs* (Checkerboard Animal Library: Dogs). Minnesota, MN: Abdo Publishing, 2010.

Websites

American Canine Association Inc., Kids Corner
www.acakids.com
Visit the official website of the American Canine Association.

National Geographic for Kids, Pet Central
kids.nationalgeographic.com/explore/pet-central/
Learn more about dogs and other pets at the official site of the National Geographic Society for Kids.

INDEX